AF573420

table of contents

# ***<u>Magic of I can</u>***
***power to overcome laziness***
***Step by step guide to be successful without hard work***

**Dop moses**

# Chapter 1

**Believe in yourself**

I'm not discussing religion or theory here. What I mean is your confidence in your capacity to succeed.

Trusting in yourself implies having confidence in your own capacities. It implies accepting that you CAN follow through with something – that it is inside your capacity. At the point when you put stock in yourself, you can defeat self-question and have the certainty to make a move and finish things.

While you're suffocating in fears, questions, and practicing self-destructive behavior ways of behaving, achievement feels beyond your control. The abilities in general, preparing, and devices on the planet won't transform you.

That is the reason I'm offering these strong moves toward defeat the hindrances in the method of your self-assurance.

If you have any desire to speed up this cycle, you can figure out how to conquer self-uncertainty and make a move (in only multi week) with our new smaller than usual course Trusting in Yourself. Begin your excursion today!

5 Moves toward Certainly Putting stock in Yourself
When you set your confidence in yourself, achievement is 100 percent feasible for you.

1. Work on your assets (not shortcomings)
step by step instructions to find lasting success center around qualities

At the point when you bomb again and again at something that appears simple to other people, trusting in yourself is almost unimaginable.

Battling with certainty, you will generally zero in on things you can't do. That is on the grounds that you feel shortcomings all the more definitely. They are agonizingly featured in your brain, images of disgrace, shortcoming, and disappointment.

"I'm terrible at this," rapidly heightens to, "I won't ever be great at anything!"

Fortunately everybody has shortcomings — and qualities.

You really want to decide how to distinguish your assets, so you can get the most mileage out of them.

The answer for begin building certainty immediately:

Quit wasting your time at things you're not wired for.

Find what you are now great at, and work at becoming perfect.

A typical propensity for fruitful individuals is to zero in on the positive — what they succeed at — and delegate shortcomings to others as opposed to stressing over not having the right stuff.

At the point when you shift your concentration to fostering your assets, you will easily feel more able and certain. What's more, when you put exertion into fostering your innate capacities, you can turn into a boss.

Perhaps you know a portion of your assets. To get a few thoughts, ponder how individuals could portray you:

Continuously has a fabulous vision, 10,000 foot view thinking
Sees the easily overlooked details, thorough
Loves learning and examination
Great communicator
Never surrenders
Hands on and activity arranged
Converse with your family, dear companions, and partners about what your assets are. What are a few things they come to you for assistance with? You're not looking for validation, however once in a while this exercise can accompany a certain help.

In the event that you don't have the foggiest idea what your assets
You're perfect at promoting yet horrendous with numbers. Rethink your accounting, and recruit an expert to deal with the spending plan.
You sparkle at making content however fear connecting via online entertainment. Use robotization devices to share your work, or recruit a specialist.

You love higher perspective preparation, yet get adhered when now is the ideal time to carry out. Take on an accomplice who can get your thoughts going.
Utilize your assets for your potential benefit. This approach will draw out your certainty as you center around utilizing your best abilities. Moving all the other things off of your plate enables you to be wonderful at what you excel at.

Your assets make you exceptional. Foster these characteristics and rely upon them.

2. Be your own mentor
put stock in-yourself-mentor

In the event that you don't put stock in yourself, you will have a hard time believing somebody who is giving a shout out to you from the sidelines. That is the reason an incredible private company mentor drives their clients to progress not by cheerleading, however by creating ability.

As per Gallup's exploration, extraordinary execution is a consequence of directors who engage workers. Chiefs who center around creating ability obtain extraordinary outcomes.

Incredible mentors, and directors, lead by enabling individuals to prevail with the right devices, training, and assets to become phenomenal. They associate with individuals utilizing approaches like Conversational Knowledge to reassure individuals and draw out the best in everybody.

The examination shows that positive reasoning, objective setting, and execution surveys don't make results all alone. At the point when you don't really accept that you have the stuff, those things are generally not an enchanted shot.

So how might you exploit this information, and mentor yourself?

Search out the apparatuses and training to foster your ability. Make a move.

Each step you take, drawing nearer to your objective, is proof of your capacity to succeed. Putting stock in yourself will become simpler and simpler, the more you see your prosperity reflected back to you.

The mystery is, you needn't bother with someone else to manage this interaction. You don't have to have characteristics of authority to mentor yourself through it.

Try to look further into yourself without being critical.

Begin by journaling on where you need to be throughout everyday life. Work out everything you need to have, and the sort of individual you need to be. From this, you can think of procedures to arrive at that point.

What does achievement resemble for you?

Picking thoughts that suit you — and working with your assets — can impel you towards your own vision of progress.

You can likewise work out the pieces of your life that you're discontent with. Make activity steps, and track down the assets, to work on any of these areas:

Feeling overpowered with liabilities
Needing more reason throughout everyday life
Hankering all the more extra energy for things you love (perusing, planting, climbing)
Worry about funds
By recognizing the pieces of your life that you're least happy with and watching out for where you eventually need to be, make long haul objectives that are sensible for you.

Put forth each major objective in turn, and separate it into more modest parts. Prevailing with regards to making every little move step, regardless of how small, prompts noticeable advancement.

At last, these reliable little victories amount to self-conviction and huge certainty.

Over the long haul, you begin to see that you can accomplish anything you set your attention to — on the grounds that you are as of now getting it done.

3. Embrace what your identity is
trust in-yourself-act naturally

How might you have confidence in yourself when you don't have the foggiest idea who you truly are? Or then again more awful, you are making a respectable attempt to be somebody else.

Self-assurance comes from embracing what your identity is and what means a lot to you. It doesn't come from being inauthentic or attempting to dazzle individuals.

Not exactly simple or easy.

The strain to fit in, to "be typical," is solid, and it begins early. That is fine to carry on with an unexceptional life. In any case, you're here, perusing this article, since that is not an ideal life for you. You need something else.

To begin accepting you can have the existence you need, you should dig profoundly to find what that will resemble for you. You should comprehend what makes you interesting, and commend those things.

At the point when you start living consistent with your character and guiding principle, you will begin putting stock in your value, your capacities, and your human potential. Fundamental beliefs are the establishment for shaping your own way of thinking to direct your activities going ahead.

Embracing yourself is best finished in gradual steps:

Begin by recording what means a lot to you.
You'll believe you should do this multiple times over weeks, or even months. Each time you'll draw nearer to revealing your fundamental beliefs.

This will assist you with seeing through the things you've been adapted to have faith in. At the point when you're done, you'll have a rundown of qualities that address your most genuine self.

Notice your examples of thought and conduct.
the most effective method to have faith in-yourself-notice

Do you frequently take special care of others to the detriment of your own qualities? At the point when you believe you're being great or maintaining order, wonder why. The final product is that you dull your own sparkle and live for others' endorsement.

At the point when you feel this struggle under the surface occurring, work on tending to it. You can sympathetically say no, declare an alternate assessment, or let somebody in on what they've done has harmed you.

Certain individuals probably won't like the "enhanced you," and that is Completely fine. They can assume a more restricted part in your life. Luckily, when you're truly you, the perfect individuals will be attracted to you, and genuine kinships will develop significantly further.

Step out from the assumptions for other people.
Being legitimate feels like a major gamble, and you may fear analysis. Recollect that your experience of life is about you, and their experience of life is about them.

Doing things that alarm you will cement the certainty you should be your most genuine self. It sounds irrational, yet being defenseless – tolerating your trepidation and not concealing it – is the surest way to develop fortitude.

Set aside a few minutes for experiences that are all the way out of your ordinary daily practice. It very well may be leaping out of a plane, taking a wellness class, or getting a paintbrush. Pick something that appears to be fun however startles you to some extent a smidgen and hop in.

You can find out such a huge amount about yourself from these exercises that you ought to participate in them consistently. Mix it up and do new things frequently.

4. Accept you can and you will
the most effective method to put stock in-yourself

Your conviction is the absolute most integral asset you have. You can totally change your life by simply changing your convictions.

It's not living in fantasy land – accepting something has an impact on the manner in which you see the world and yourself.

You either see prospects, or difficult deterrents.

Which will you pick?

To begin putting stock in yourself, you need to quit accepting you are left with the abilities and capacities you have at the present time. This is known as a decent mentality, which is a restricted reasoning example that is lethal to your prosperity.

All things considered, begin accepting you can change. This perspective is known as a development outlook. It implies that you accept change as conceivable.

The facts may demonstrate that you don't have the stuff to achieve your objectives

# Chapter 2

**Be bold**

On the off chance that you're never striking in your life, you'll find it hard to battle for what you put stock in. Carrying on with a daily existence consistent with yourself implies that you need to support what you trust in. This implies you must be strong once in a while. In any case, how might you really become bolder?

Being strong doesn't mean crushing pens at your partners at whatever point they can't help contradicting you and pitching a fit. All things considered, you need to be deferential and self-assured when you're strong. Contingent upon your character, this can be challenging. Be that as it may, the advantages of being strong far offset the expected adverse results.

In the event that defending yourself and being strong sounds like a bad dream to you, you're perfectly located. This article shows you why it means a lot to be strong in your life, with significant hints to assist you with getting everything rolling,
Being strong can be hard. Particularly in the event that you're an individual that values harmony and attempts to stay away from struggle consistently.

For what reason is it critical to be striking? This statement summarizes it rather pleasantly.

In the event that you have no foes in life you have never supported anything.

Winston Churchill
Being strong signifies "not wavering or unfortunate in that frame of mind of genuine or conceivable risk or rebuke". This frequently means defending what you put stock in, notwithstanding possibly stepping on somebody's toe.

For instance, envision you're in a gathering at work and everyone around you settles on something that you don't have confidence in. Assuming that you're striking, you'd support your viewpoint and put forth your defense.

Regardless of whether it implies that you need to discredit your partners.
Regardless of whether it implies the gathering will accept two times as lengthy.
Also, regardless of whether your supervisor will need to talk with you subsequently.
All in all, being strong means making some noise or misbehaving, without harping on the possible unfortunate results of your activities.

What being strong doesn't mean
Being intense may be viewed as something to be thankful for, however on the off chance that you go excessively far, you'll not exclusively be strong yet you may likewise be mean, rude, and imprudent.

These are things that you ought to be careful about. All things considered, you ought to attempt to be strong in a positive manner:

By being confident in your correspondence, yet all at once not harmful.
By continuously regarding the assessment of another person.
By not allowing your feelings to get the high ground, and following level headedness all things being equal.
How can you say whether you've been excessively strong? You can frequently get very smart thought from individuals you're with.

At the point when individuals give you certain input and they keep on requesting your perspective, you've likely worked effectively.

In the event that, then again, you're not welcome to gatherings any longer, odds are you've crossed the line.

Why it's essential to be striking some of the time
As examined, choosing to be striking might bring about a few adverse results. At the point when you say no, contradict some common norms, or challenge the standard in light of what you really have confidence in, you might confront dismissal or counter.

Notwithstanding, when you're justified and you in the long run track down the mental fortitude to make some noise, it tends to very compensate. It might help you:

Get others to regard you more
Give a voice to the mistreated.
Escape what is happening.
Have a genuine effect locally.
Get what you genuinely merit.
Unite individuals.
A portion of these advantages are even upheld by studies.

Being intense can expand your certainty
It frequently seems like certainty and strength remain closely connected. All things considered, how might you be striking in the event that you're not sure and don't have confidence in yourself?

Be that as it may, does certainty prompt strength, or is it the opposite way around? A recent report tracked down a huge positive connection between emphatic way of behaving and confidence in young people. In spite of the fact that it's muddled which started things out, high confidence or self-assured conduct, the connection between them is evident.

Being intense can give a voice to the persecuted
It takes just a single intense individual to motivate a gathering to stand up.

The best illustration of this that I am aware of is the #MeToo development. This development ignited an insurgency among ladies who have encountered various types of inappropriate behavior and hadn't tracked down the fortitude to shout out up to that point.

In the event that you've been physically irritated or attacked, compose 'me too' as an answer to this tweet. pic.twitter.com/k2oeCiUf9n

This is a lovely illustration of how it might just take one striking individual to cause an adjustment of the world. By being striking, you'll be bound to influence the world for the better as a matter of fact.

6 methods for being bolder throughout everyday life

At this point, it ought to be certain that being strong accompanies a ton of advantages (and a few expected traps).

Yet, how might you really become bolder throughout everyday life, particularly when this doesn't appear to be important for what your identity is? The following are 6 methods for being strong throughout everyday life, no matter what your character type.

1. Track down your qualities throughout everyday life

It's a lot simpler to be striking in the event that you understand a big motivator for you. Being strong and shouting out frequently begins from sorting out and characterizing your qualities.

There are numerous approaches to this. For instance, you can essentially attempt to conceptualize and record ways of behaving and attributes that you esteem in yourself as well as other people. Yet, on a more unambiguous level, you can likewise record your objectives for a task at work. In the event that you understand what your objectives and values are, it'll be more straightforward to support yourself at whatever point it's required.

The main thing to know is to take as need might arise and be totally genuine with yourself. Remember that qualities in various areas of life can some of the time go against one another: you might esteem freedom in your own life and participation at work or the other way around.

You may likewise find that your qualities don't totally line up with those of your partners or good examples. Be encouraged in the event that these things occur: you're sorting out your own qualities, not another person's.

2. Keep yourself informed

While being striking and decisive is something positive, you would rather not be known as an intense, clueless and innocent individual. Assuming that occurs, being striking abruptly loses its allure, correct?

In the event that you go to bat for yourself and be strong, it's vital to be educated about anything you're doing. In the event that you're in a gathering and present a defense about something that conflicts with your partners, you better ensure you can deal with a touch of opposition.

The more educated you are, the more sure you can be in agreeing with a particular position or holding fast. You are additionally less vulnerable to lack of regard, antagonism, and dismissal assuming that you have the real factors fixed.

It means a lot to not simply search for data that upholds your perspective. Investigating the counter-arguments is seemingly considerably more significant. How could somebody contradict what you trust in? At the point when you're appropriately educated on pretty much every one of the points, you'll be better ready to defend yourself without being quieted by the resistance.

This likewise assists you with relieving the majority of the dangers that accompany being intense. On the off chance that you're attempting to be strong without being educated, you might appear to be foolish.

3. Say no

Up until this point, we've discussed knowing your qualities and keeping yourself informed. These things are significant bits of the riddle, however they don't really make you strong.

Here's something that assists you with being bolder throughout everyday life: say no on a more regular basis.

You should understand that "No" is a finished sentence.

On the off chance that somebody asks you something that you're not obliged to do and don't have any desire to do, you can essentially say "No" and leave it at that. You don't necessarily need to legitimize why you can't come to a party, or why you can't stay at work past 40 hours at the end of the week.

By turning out to be more OK with saying "No", you'll view it simpler as more consistent with yourself. In James Altucher's book The Force of No, he affirms that the adage "No" more frequently is truly saying "OK" to your own life. A life that is more significant for you. While an excess of 'yes' can pass on us emptied genuinely and actually out of overcommitment to other people.

In the event that you believe more tips on how could say no on a more regular basis, you might like our article on the most proficient method to quit being an accommodating person.

4. Figure out how to determine clashes as opposed to staying away from them

Individuals might be furious or frustrated in you when you say no, particularly assuming they're utilized to you saying OK. Feelings, even pessimistic ones, are a characteristic piece of human connections. A decent relationship isn't really one without struggle, but instead one where clashes are settled.

It isn't your work and obligation to keep others blissful.

On the off chance that somebody resents you or has harmed and offended you, address the issue. Express the issue and your sentiments about it and let the other individual give their opinion. Use "I" explanations and try not to cause suppositions about how the other individual could to feel.

For instance: "I could have done without how you settled on the choice without examining it with me first." or "I can see that you are furious with me. You were depending on me to show up with your arrangement and I didn't."

This is an incredible way to not exclusively be strong, yet additionally emphatic and deferential towards others.

5. Come clean

A significant stage in carrying on with a striking life is, obviously, coming clean.

In the event that you don't find something entertaining, then don't chuckle.
On the off chance that you disagree with what somebody says, then, at that point, don't.
This John Lennon quote summarizes it actually pleasantly:

Being straightforward may not get you a great deal of companions however it'll constantly get you the right ones.

John Lennon

By not being certifiable, you start a chain response of exploitative endorsement of what you loathe, empowering a greater amount of it later on. Along these lines, you can assist with making a climate in your life that you could do without. It's like obliging a shade of blue for the parlor that you're not really that enthused about.

This intently lines up with our article on carrying on with a day to day existence consistent with yourself, which contains more tips like this one!

6. Embrace the uneasiness

Assuming you've never supported yourself or said no, offering your actual viewpoints can be terrifying. In any case, to develop and learn, you must escape your usual range of familiarity.

For instance, when someone requests that you follow through with something and you reply "No", I

# Chapter 3

# Don't be lazy

An absence of enthusiasm for your work, a mind-boggling plan for the day, and, surprisingly, a fundamental ailment are only a portion of the things that can impede your craving to finish things.

Instructions to conquer lethargy
"How might I stop apathy?" The response may not be all around as simple as you'd anticipate. While certain individuals might be more inclined to being apathetic than others, even exceptionally useful individuals can find it trying to finish things here and there.

Here are a few hints to assist you with disposing of sluggishness and get a grip on your efficiency.

1. Make your objectives sensible
Laying out ridiculous objectives and taking on a lot of can prompt burnout. While not a genuine clinical conclusion, the side effects of burnout are perceived by clinical experts. Work burnout can cause fatigue, loss of interest and inspiration, and a yearning to get away.

Abstain from over-burdening by setting more modest, achievable objectives that will get you where you need to be without overpowering you en route.

2. Try not to anticipate that yourself should be awesome
Compulsiveness is on the ascent and it's incurring significant damage.

One 2017 review that checked out at undergrads somewhere in the range of 1989 and 2016 tracked down an expansion in compulsiveness throughout the long term. Analysts noted "youngsters [are] now confronting more serious conditions, more ridiculous assumptions, and more restless and controlling guardians than ages previously."

This ascent in hairsplitting is making individuals be excessively condemning of themselves as well as other people. It's additionally prompted an expansion in discouragement and nervousness.

One more modest investigation of undergrads inferred that expecting flawlessness was connected with avoidant adapting, which makes you try not to manage stressors.

3. Utilize positive rather than negative self-talk
Negative self-talk can crash your endeavors to finish things in each part of your life. Letting yourself know that you're a lethargic individual is a type of negative self-talk.

You can stop your negative inside voice by rehearsing positive self-talk. Rather than saying, "It's basically impossible that I can finish this," say, "I'll do my absolute best with it to get it going."

4. Make a game plan
Arranging how you will finish something can make it simpler to arrive. Be sensible about how long, exertion, and different variables are expected to meet your objective and make an activity plan. Having an arrangement will give guidance and certainty that can help regardless of whether you hit an obstacle en route.

5. Utilize your assets
Pause for a minute to contemplate what your assets are while getting objectives positioned outfitting to handle an errand. Attempt to apply them to various parts of an errand to assist you with finishing things. Research has shown that zeroing in on qualities increments efficiency, good sentiments, and commitment to work.

6. Perceive your achievements en route
Congratulating yourself for an expert piece of handiwork can assist with persuading you to continue onward. Consider recording each of your achievements en route in all that you do, whether at work or home. It's an extraordinary method for helping your certainty and energy, and fueling you to continue.

7. Request help
Many individuals accept that requesting help is an indication of shortcoming. In any case, not requesting help could be setting you up for disappointment. A 2018 studyTrusted

Source discovered that individuals who don't ask colleagues for help were bound to be disappointed in their positions and had lower levels of occupation execution. They were likewise seen less well by their managers.

Requesting help works on your odds of coming out on top and assists you with associating with other people who can support and rouse you.

8. Keep away from interruption

We as a whole have our number one interruptions we go to when we're simply not wanting to do an errand – whether it's looking at online entertainment or playing with a pet.

Track down ways of making your interruptions less available. This can mean tracking down a tranquil work environment, similar to the library or a vacant room, or utilizing an application to hinder locales that you scroll carelessly when you ought to be on task.

9. Make dreary assignments fun

We will more often than not stay away from occupations that we see as exhausting or dreary. Tasks like cleaning the drains or restroom won't ever be heaps of tomfoolery, yet you can make them more agreeable. Take a stab at listening to music or a digital broadcast, or put on your wellness tracker to perceive the number of calories you consume or steps you get while playing out these undertakings.

10. Reward yourself

Finishing a task is a compensation in itself, yet certain individuals are driven by outer prizes. Center around what you'll acquire from finishing something, such as drawing nearer to an advancement, or prize yourself for an incredible piece of handiwork. Praise the finish of a major task with an evening out on the town or welcome companions over for drink following a day of cleanings

11 the mind is engaged with all that we do and, similar to some other piece of the body, it should be really focused on as well.

Practicing the cerebrum to further develop memory, concentration, or day to day usefulness is a first concern for some individuals, particularly as they progress in years. All things considered, individuals, everything being equal, can profit from integrating a couple of basic mind practices into their everyday existence, which we'll investigate in more detail in this article.

Cerebrum works out

Research has shown that there are numerous ways you can sharpen your smartness and assist your cerebrum with remaining solid, regardless of what age you are. Doing specific mind activities to assist with helping your memory, fixation, and center can make day to day errands speedier and more straightforward to do, and keep your cerebrum sharp as you progress in years.

We should bring a more profound jump into 11 proof based practices that offer the best mind helping benefits.

1. Mess around with a jigsaw puzzle
Whether you're assembling a 1,000-piece picture of the Eiffel Pinnacle or joining 100 parts to make Mickey Mouse, dealing with a jigsaw puzzle is a magnificent method for reinforcing your cerebrum.

ResearchTrusted Source has shown that doing jigsaw puzzles selects different mental capacities and is a defensive component for visuospatial mental maturing. As such, while assembling a jigsaw puzzle, you need to take a gander at various pieces and sort out where they fit inside the bigger picture. This can be an extraordinary method for testing and exercise your mind.

2. Take a stab at cards
When's the last time you played a round of cards?
Source on intellectually invigorating exercises for grown-ups, say a fast game can prompt more noteworthy mind volume in a few districts of the cerebrum. A similar report likewise found that a round of cards could further develop memory and thinking abilities.

Have a go at learning one of these reliable games:

solitaire
span
gin rummy
poker
hearts
insane eights

3. Assemble your jargon

A rich jargon has an approach to making you sound savvy. Yet, did you realize you can likewise transform a fast vocab illustration into an invigorating mind game?

Research shows that a lot more districts of the mind are engaged with jargon errands, especially in regions that are significant for visual and hear-able handling. To test this hypothesis, attempt this mental helping action:

Keep a scratch pad with you when you read.
Record one new word, then look into the definition.
Attempt to utilize that word multiple times the following day.

4. Dance your heart out

The Communities for Sickness Avoidance and Control noticed that learning new dance moves can build your mind's handling velocity and memory. All in all, make something happen on the dance floor and your mind will be obliged.

Need to test it out? Check one of these dance exercises out:

Take a salsa, tap, hip-bounce, or contemporary dance class.
Attempt a Zumba or jazz practice class.
Watch an internet based video with fun dance moves you've for a long time truly needed to learn.
Snatch an accomplice and figure out how couples dance.
Accumulate your companions and go line moving.

5. Utilize every one of your faculties

A 2015 examination reportTrusted Source proposes that utilizing every one of your faculties might assist with reinforcing your cerebrum.

To give your faculties and your cerebrum an exercise, have a go at doing exercises that all the while connect every one of the five of your faculties. You could have a go at baking a bunch of treats, visiting a rancher's market, or attempting another eatery while you center around smelling, contacting, tasting, seeing, and hearing all simultaneously.

6. Get familiar with another ability
Mastering another ability isn't just tomfoolery and fascinating, yet it might likewise assist with reinforcing the associations in your cerebrum.

Research from 2014 Trusted Source likewise demonstrates the way that mastering another expertise can assist with further developing memory capability in more seasoned grown-ups.

Is there something you've for a long time needed to figure out how to do? Maybe you might want to know how to fix your vehicle, utilize a specific programming system, or ride a pony? You presently have another valid justification to discover that new ability.

7. Show another ability to another person
One of the most mind-blowing ways of extending your mastering is to show an expertise to someone else.

After you get familiar with another expertise, you want to rehearse it. Instructing it to another person expects you to make sense of the idea and right any errors you make. For instance, figure out how to swing a golf club, then, at that point, show the moves toward a companion.

8. Pay attention to or play music
Do you believe that a simple way should build your inventive intellectual prowess? The response might lie in turning on some music.

As per a 2017 studyTrusted Source, paying attention to blissful tunes produces more imaginative arrangements contrasted with being peaceful. And that implies, wrenching up some vibe great music can assist with helping your imaginative reasoning and mental ability.

What's more, if you need to figure out how to play music, this present time is an extraordinary opportunity to begin on the grounds that your cerebrum is equipped for mastering new abilities anytime in your life. That is the reason you're never excessively old to begin playing an instrument like the piano, guitar, or even the drums.

9. Take another course
Try not to become trapped in a hopeless cycle with regards to your day to day errands. All things being equal, attempt better approaches to do exactly the same things.

Pick an alternate course to get to work every week or attempt an alternate method of transport, such as trekking or utilizing public vehicles as opposed to driving. Your mind can profit from this straightforward change, and you may be astonished by the fact that changing your thinking is so natural.

10. Think
Day to dayContemplate
Everyday contemplation can quiet your body, slow your breathing, and lessen pressure and uneasiness.

In any case, did you have any idea that it might likewise help adjust your memory and increment your cerebrum's capacity to deal with informationTrusted Source?

Track down a peaceful spot, shut your eyes, and go through five minutes reflecting every day.

11. Get familiar with another dialect
A 2012 survey of researchTrusted Source has predominantly demonstrated the numerous mental advantages of having the option to communicate in more than one language.

As per various investigations, bilingualism can add to better memory, worked on visual-spatial abilities, and more significant levels of imagination. Being conversant in more than one language may likewise assist you with exchanging all the more effectively between various errands, and defer the beginning old enough related cognitive deterioration.

Fortunately receiving the benefits of learning another language is rarely past the point of no return. As per specialists, you can support your memory and work on other mental capabilities by turning into an understudy of another dialect whenever in your life.

12. Take up kendo

Its an obvious fact that judo can help your wellbeing in numerous ways, including your psychological well-being. Besides, it can likewise assist with focusing you when life appears to be out of equilibrium.

Taking up a customary act of jujitsu can assist with lessening pressure, improve rest quality, and further develop memory. A 2013 studyTrusted Source discovered that drawn out jujitsu training could prompt underlying changes in the cerebrum, bringing about an expansion in mind volume.

Fledglings truly do best by taking a class to become familiar with the various developments. In any case, when you know the rudiments, you can rehearse judo anyplace, whenever.

13. Center around someone else

The following time you interface with somebody, observe four things about them. Perhaps you notice the shade of their shirt or jeans. Might it be said that they are wearing glasses? Do they have a cap on, and provided that this is true, what sort of cap? What tone is their hair?

When you settle on four things to recall, give careful consideration, and return to it later in the day. Record what you recollect about those four subtleties.

The reality

Zeroing in on your mind's wellbeing is perhaps everything thing you can manage to work on your fixation, concentration, memory, and mental deftness, regardless of what age you are. By integrating cerebrum practices into your daily existence, you'll get to challenge your brain, improve your mental abilities, and conceivably discover some new information and advancing en route, as well

# Chapter 4

## Objective setting

The most effective method to Put forth an Objective
First consider what you need to accomplish, and afterward focus on it. Set Savvy (explicit, quantifiable, feasible, significant and time-bound) objectives that persuade you and record them to cause them to feel substantial. Then plan the means you should take to understand your objective, and cross off every one as you work through them.

Objective setting is a strong cycle for pondering your optimal future, and for spurring yourself to transform your vision of this future into the real world.

The most common way of putting forth objectives assists you with picking where you need to go throughout everyday life. By knowing unequivocally what you need to accomplish, you know where you need to think about your endeavors. You'll likewise rapidly detect the interruptions that can, with such ease, mislead you.

Why Laid out Objectives?
High level competitors, fruitful money managers and achievers in all fields generally put forth objectives. Putting forth objectives gives you long haul vision and momentary inspiration . It centers your obtaining of information, and assists you with putting together your time and your assets so you can take advantage of your life.

By setting sharp, obviously characterized objectives, you can gauge and invest heavily in the accomplishment of those objectives, and you'll see forward improvement in what could beforehand have appeared to be a long trivial drudgery. You will likewise raise your self-assurance , as you perceive your own capacity and ability in accomplishing the objectives that you've set.

Beginning to Lay out Private Objectives
You put forth your objectives on various levels:

First you make your "higher perspective" of how you need to manage your life (or over, express, the following 10 years), and distinguish the huge scope objectives that you need to accomplish.
Then, you separate these into the increasingly small focuses that you should hit to arrive at your lifetime objectives.
At last, when you have your arrangement, you begin dealing with it to accomplish these objectives.
For this reason we start the method involved with laying out objectives by checking out at your lifetime objectives. Then, we work down to the things that you can do in, express, the following five years, then, at that point, one year from now, one month from now, one week from now, and today, to begin moving towards them.

Stage 1: Putting forth Lifetime Objectives
The most vital phase in defining individual objectives is to consider what you need to accomplish in the course of your life (or possibly, by a critical and far off age from here on out).

Putting forth lifetime objectives gives you the general viewpoint that shapes any remaining parts of your navigation.

Finding This Article Valuable?
You can gain proficiency with one more 63 time usage abilities, similar to this, by joining the Brain Devices Club.

Join the Brain Instruments Club Today!
To give a wide, adjusted inclusion of exceedingly significant regions in your day to day existence, attempt to put forth objectives in a portion of the accompanying classes (or in different classifications of your own, where these are mean quite a bit to you):

Vocation - What level would you like to arrive at in your profession, or what is it that you need to accomplish?
Monetary - What amount would you like to acquire, by what stage? How is this connected with your vocation objectives?
Schooling - Is there any information you need to secure specifically? What data and abilities will you really want to have to accomplish different objectives?
Family - Would you like to be a parent? Provided that this is true, how can you go to be a decent parent? How would you like to be seen by an accomplice or by individuals from your more distant family?
Imaginative - Would you like to accomplish any creative objectives?
Mentality - Is any essential for your outlook keeping you down? Is there anything in particular that disturbs you? (Provided that this is true, put forth an objective to work on your way of behaving or track down an answer for the issue.)

Physical - Are there any athletic objectives that you need to accomplish, or do you need great wellbeing profound into advanced age? What steps would you say you will take to accomplish this?
Delight - How would you like to have a ball? (You ought to guarantee that a portion of your life is for you!)
Public Help - Would you like to make the world a superior place? Provided that this is true, how?
Invest some energy conceptualizing these things, and afterward select at least one objective in every class that best reflect what you need to do. Then, at that point, consider managing again so you have few truly critical objectives that you can zero in on.

As you do this, ensure that the objectives that you have set are ones that you truly need to accomplish, not ones that your folks, family, or bosses could need. (Assuming you have an accomplice, you most likely need to consider what the individual needs - nonetheless, ensure that you likewise stay consistent with yourself!)

Tip:
You may likewise need to peruse our article on Private Statements of purpose . Making an individual statement of purpose can assist with bringing your most significant objectives into sharp concentration.

Stage 2: Laying out More modest Objectives
Whenever you have laid out your lifetime objectives, set a five-year plan of more modest objectives that you really want

to finish on the off chance that you are to arrive at your lifetime plan.

Then, at that point, make a one-year plan, half year plan, and a one-month plan of logically more modest objectives that you ought to reach to accomplish your lifetime objectives. Each of these ought to be founded on the past arrangement.

Then make an everyday Plan for the day of things that you ought to accomplish today to pursue your lifetime objectives.

At a beginning phase, your more modest objectives may be to understand books and assemble data on the accomplishment of your more elevated level objectives. This will assist you with working on the quality and authenticity of your objective setting.

At last, survey your arrangements, and ensure that they fit the manner by which you need to carry on with your life.

Tip:
On the off chance that you feel that you're not giving sufficient consideration to specific parts of your life, you'll track down our articles on The Wheel of Life and the Life/Profession Rainbow helpful.

Keeping on track
Whenever you've settled on your most memorable arrangement of objectives, move the cycle along by evaluating and refreshing your Plan for the day consistently.

Occasionally audit the more drawn out term designs, and adjust them to mirror your changing needs and experience. (A decent approach to doing this is to plan ordinary, rehashing surveys utilizing a PC based journal.)

Shrewd Objectives

A valuable approach to making objectives all the more remarkable is to utilize the Brilliant memory helper. While there are a lot of variations (some of which we've remembered for bracket), Shrewd for the most part represents:

S - Explicit (or Huge).
M - Quantifiable (or Significant).
A - Feasible (or Activity Situated).
R - Pertinent (or Fulfilling).
T - Time-bound (or Identifiable).
For instance, rather than having "to cruise all over the planet" as an objective, utilizing the Savvy objective "To have finished my outing all over the planet by December 31, 2027." Clearly, this may be feasible in the event that a ton of readiness has been finished beforehand is all the more remarkable!

Further Ways to define Your Objectives

The accompanying wide rules will assist you with setting viable, attainable objectives:

Express every objective as a positive proclamation - Express your objectives emphatically - "Execute this procedure well" is a greatly improved objective than "Don't commit this moronic error."

Be exact - Put forth exact objectives, placing in dates, times and sums so you can gauge accomplishment. Assuming you do this, you'll know precisely when you have accomplished the objective, and can take total fulfillment from having accomplished it.
Put forth boundaries - When you have a few objectives, give each vital. This assists you with abstaining from feeling overpowered by having an excessive number of objectives, and assists with guiding your focus toward the main ones.
Get objectives on paper - This solidifies them and gives them more power.
Keep functional objectives little - Keep the low-level objectives that you're making progress toward little and feasible. In the event that an objective is excessively huge, it can appear to be that you are not gaining ground towards it. Saving objectives little and gradual offers more chances for remuneration.
Put forth execution objectives, not result objectives - You ought to take care to lay out objectives over which you have however much control as could be expected. It tends to be very crippling to neglect to accomplish an individual objective because of reasons outside of your reach!

In business, these reasons could be awful business conditions or unforeseen impacts of government strategy. In sport, they could incorporate unfortunate judging, awful climate, injury, or outright misfortune.

On the off chance that you base your objectives on private execution, you can keep command over the accomplishment of your objectives, and draw fulfillment from them.

Put forth practical objectives - Defining objectives that you can achieve is significant. A wide range of individuals (for instance, bosses, guardians, media, or society) can lay out ridiculous objectives for you. They will frequently do this in obliviousness of your own cravings and aspirations.

It's likewise conceivable to define objectives that are too troublesome in light of the fact that you probably won't see the value in either the impediments in the way, or see very how much expertise you really want to create to accomplish a specific degree of execution.

Accomplishing Objectives

At the point when you've accomplished an objective, find an opportunity to partake in the fulfillment of having done as such. Ingest the ramifications of the objective accomplishment, and notice the headway that you've made towards different objectives.

In the event that the objective was a huge one, reward yourself properly. Each of this assists you with building the fearlessness you merit.

With the experience of having accomplished this objective, audit the remainder of your objective plans:

On the off chance that you accomplished the objective too effectively, make your next objective harder.

On the off chance that the objective required some investment to accomplish, make the following objective somewhat simpler.

Assuming you mastered something that would lead you to change different objectives, do as such.
On the off chance that you saw a shortage in your abilities notwithstanding accomplishing the objective, choose whether to define objectives to fix this.
Tip 1:
Our article, Brilliant Guidelines of Objective Setting , will tell you the best way to put yourself in a good position with regards to your objectives. In the event that you're actually experiencing difficulty, you could likewise need to attempt In reverse Objective Setting .

Tip 2:
It's memorable critical that neglecting to meet objectives doesn't make any difference much, similarly as long as you gain from the experience.

Feed examples you have learned once more into the most common way of laying out your next objectives. Recollect that your objectives will change over the long haul. cycle of laying out your next objectives. Recall too that your objectives will change over the long haul. Change them routinely to reflect development in your insight and experience, and in the event that objectives hold no fascination any longer, consider letting them go.

Model Individual Objectives
For her fresh new Goal, Susan has chosen to contemplate how she truly needs to manage her life.

Her lifetime objectives are as per the following:

Profession - "To oversee the supervisor of the magazine that I work for."
Imaginative - "To continue to chip away at my delineation abilities. At last I need to have my own show in our midtown exhibition."
Physical - "To run a long distance race."
Since Susan has recorded her lifetime objectives, she then, at that point, separates everyone into more modest, more reasonable objectives.

We should investigate how she could separate her lifetime profession objective - becoming overseeing manager of her magazine:

Five-year objective: "Become agent manager."
One-year objective: "Volunteer for projects that the current Overseeing Manager is going up."
Half year objective: "Return to school and complete my news-casting degree."
One-month objective: "Converse with the current supervisor to figure out what abilities are expected to finish the work."
One-week objective: "Book the gathering with the Overseeing Proofreader."
As you can see from this model, separating major objectives into more modest, more reasonable objectives makes it far simpler to perceive how the objective will get achieved.

Central issues
Objective setting is a significant strategy for:

Concluding what you need to accomplish in your life.
Isolating what's significant based on what's unessential, or an interruption.
Rousing yourself.
Building your fearlessness, in light of fruitful accomplishment of objectives.
Put forth your lifetime objectives first. Then, at that point, set a five-year plan of more modest objectives that you really want to finish assuming you are to arrive at your lifetime plan. Push the interaction along by consistently evaluating and refreshing your objectives. What's more, make sure to carve out opportunity to partake in the fulfillment of accomplishing your objectives when you do as such.

On the off chance that you don't currently lay out objectives, do as such, beginning at this point. As you make this method a piece of your life, you'll find your vocation speeding up, and you'll consider how you managed without it!

What an exquisite message from you - gratitude for offering that to us!

I concur - getting your objectives, cycle, and progress on paper is very strong. I feel that it gives me an alternate point of view on my own choices and so on - it's as though the "distance" that the diary manages the cost of me from my own cerebrum and psyche, assists me with being more goal.
It's additionally fascinating to see, assuming you read back in your own diary, the amount you've developed and what your different points of view were.

# Chapter 5

**Set aside some cash**

This is the way we bring in cash.

With regards to setting aside cash, little changes can add up rapidly. Changing a couple of day to day propensities, cutting month to month bills and utilizing devices that robotize investment funds can on the whole have a major effect.

We featured probably the most ideal ways to set aside cash immediately. These cash tips can assist you with putting something aside for a house or a vehicle or just set aside more cash out of your compensation.

21 cash saving tips

1. Robotize moves.

2. Count your coins and bills.

3. Prep for shopping for food.

4. Limit café spending.

5. Get limits on diversion.

6. Map out significant buys.

7. Confine internet shopping.

8. Defer buys with the 30-day rule.

9. Get imaginative with gifts.

10. Bring down your vehicle costs.

11. Decrease your gas use.

12. Pack link and web.

13. Switch your cell plan.

14. Decrease your electric bill.

15. Bring down your understudy loan installments.

16. Drop pointless memberships.

17. Renegotiate your home loan.

18. Put forth investment funds objectives.

19. Track spending.

20. Take care of exorbitant interest obligation.

21. Keep reserve funds in a high return investment account.

1. Mechanize moves
By setting up programmed moves from your financial records to your bank account every month, the cash will collect after some time with next to no extra work on your part. This method can be particularly helpful when your investment accounts are devoted to explicit objectives, for example, laying out a backup stash, going on a get-away or building an initial installment.

You can likewise let applications like Digit or Qapital do a portion of the work for you. After you join, they'll move modest quantities from your financial records to a different bank account for you. Like that, you don't need to invest time or energy pondering making an exchange. You can become familiar with applications that robotize investment funds and choose if they're ideal for you.

2. Count your coins and bills
Another choice is saving your change physically by putting it to the side every evening. After you have a sizable sum, you can store it straightforwardly into your reserve funds and watch your record develop from that point. As a matter of fact, when you need to watch your spending, it's smart to utilize cash rather than Mastercards on the grounds that it very well may be more earnestly to leave behind actual cash. While this technique doesn't fabricate investment funds for the time

being, it's a strong methodology for gradual reserve funds development.

3. Prep for shopping for food

A little work before you go to the supermarket can go far toward assisting you with getting a good deal on food. Check your storage space and make a shopping rundown to stay away from motivation purchasing something you needn't bother with. Figure out how to get coupons and join dependability projects to expand your investment funds as you shop. In return for sharing your telephone number or email address, your neighborhood store's steadfastness program could offer extra limits.

On the off chance that you utilize a money back Mastercard, you could make additional money back on basic food item buys. A few cards offer however much 5% or 6% money back, yet you'll need to make certain to cover off your bill every month to try not to pay revenue and charges.

The application Flipp pulls in coupons from nearby stores when you enter your Postal district. Like that, you can shop deals without figuring out the paper. On the off chance that you look for food at an enormous retailer like Objective, Amazon or Walmart, you can frequently track down extra reserve funds by downloading the store's application.

4. Limit café spending

One of the most straightforward costs to slice when you need to save more is eatery dinners, since eating out will in general be pricier than cooking at home. If you would in any case like to eat at cafés, attempt to diminish the recurrence and exploit Mastercards that reward café spending. You can likewise choose tidbits or split a dish with your feasting ally to set aside cash when you eat out. Skipping beverages and sweet can assist with extending your spending plan too.

5. Get limits on amusement

You can exploit free days at exhibition halls and public parks to save money on diversion costs. Your neighborhood local area could offer free shows and other face to face or virtual occasions; actually look at your nearby schedule prior to going overboard on expensive passes to private occasions. You can likewise get some information about limits for more seasoned grown-ups, understudies, military individuals and that's just the beginning.

6. Map out significant buys

You can save by timing your acquisition of apparatuses, furniture, vehicles, hardware and more as indicated by yearly deal periods. It's likewise worth affirming that an arrangement is really an arrangement by following costs after some time. You can allow apparatuses to do this step for you; the Camelizer program expansion tracks costs on Amazon and can make you aware of cost drops. The Honey program augmentation pulls in coupon codes and checks at lower costs somewhere else.

While you're shopping face to face, ensure you get the best arrangement by utilizing the ShopSavvy application. It allows you to filter standardized tags and cautions you to better costs somewhere else.

7. Confine internet shopping

You can make it more challenging to shop online to quit burning through cash on things you may not require. Rather than saving your charging data, pick to include your transportation address and Mastercard number each time you request. You'll presumably make less drive buys due to the additional work included.

Before you construct a spending plan

NerdWallet separates your spending and shows you ways of saving.

Back to top

8. Postpone buys with the 30-day rule

One method for trying not to overspend is to give yourself a chilling period between the time a thing grabs your attention and when you really make the buy. Assuming that you're shopping on the web, consider placing the thing in your shopping basket and afterward leaving until you've had additional opportunity to thoroughly consider it. (At times, you could try and get a coupon code when the retailer sees you deserted the truck.) On the off chance that 30 days seems like too lengthy to even consider pausing, you can attempt more limited periods like a 24-or 48-hour delay.

9. Get imaginative with gifts

You can set aside cash with reasonable gift thoughts, similar to spice gardens and books, or go the DIY course. Baking treats, making craftsmanship or setting someone up supper can show that you care similarly as much as making a costly buy, and maybe significantly more so. You can likewise give somebody the endowment of your time by proposing to take them to a neighborhood (free) gallery or other occasion.

10. Bring down your vehicle costs

Renegotiating your car credit and exploiting lower financing costs could save you impressively over the existence of your advance. Looking for vehicle insurance consistently can likewise assist you with reducing expenses contrasted and essentially letting your ongoing contract auto-restore. You can reduce vehicle upkeep expenses by driving less, eliminating weighty things from your trunk and staying away from pointless fast speed increases.

11. Lessen your gas utilization

You have zero control over costs at the siphon, however you can complete a few things to cut your gas use and set aside cash. Take a stab at utilizing a gas application to stay thrifty when you really do top off.

12. Group link and web

You could bring down your link bill by as much as $40 each month by changing your link bundle. Also, you could save more than $1,000 north of two years by packaging your link and network access, contingent upon your transporter. One more choice to consider is cutting links or if nothing else, cutting a portion of your extra real time features or premium memberships.

13. Switch your mobile phone plan

Changing your arrangement is one cash saving tip for your PDA bill, yet it's not by any means the only way. Eliminating protection from your arrangement could save you almost $100 each year, per line. Pursuing autopay and paperless explanations can save you an extra $5 to $10 each month, per line. We contrasted different wireless plans with assistance you track down the best counterpart for you.

14. Decrease your electric bill
Of all shapes and sizes changes in your energy use can assist you with saving hundreds every year on your electric bill. Consider stopping any protection spills in your home, utilizing shrewd plug extensions, trading in additional energy-proficient machines and changing to a savvy indoor regulator. Indeed, even gradual drops in your month to month power utilization can amount to huge reserve funds over the long haul.

15. Bring down your understudy loan installments
Signing up for money driven reimbursement could bring down your regularly scheduled installments to a sensible level since the sum you pay is attached to your profit. Different choices incorporate renegotiating, signing up for autopay to set off a rebate, and making additional installments so you can empty the obligation quicker, what cuts the general interest you'll pay.

16 the auto-restablish choice on any memberships you're not utilizing routinely, for example, membership boxes. You could try and pay for memberships you never again use or need. Checking on your Mastercard or bank proclamation cautiously

can assist you with hailing any repetitive costs you can dispose of. Furthermore, try not to pursue free preliminaries that require installment data, or possibly make a note or set a schedule suggestion to drop before the free period closes.

17. Renegotiate your home loan

Renegotiating your home loan can save you a few hundred bucks every month in the event that you're ready to catch a lower financing cost. Utilize our home loan renegotiate adding machine to figure out the amount you could save. While renegotiating accompanies a few introductory expenses forthright, they can be recovered over the long run, when you begin paying less every month.

18. Put forth reserve funds objectives

Put forth a particular yet practical objective. It might very well be "save $5,000 in a singular retirement account this year" or "pay off my Visa obligation quicker." Utilize a reserve funds objective mini-computer to perceive the amount of you'd possess to save every month or year to arrive at your objective.

Back to top

19. Track spending

Monitor your month to month income — your pay less your consumptions. This step will likewise gain it simpler to stamp headway toward your investment funds objective. Attempt a financial plan application that tracks your spending. (NerdWallet has a free application that does exactly that.) Or you can follow these five moves toward assist with following your month to month expenses.

20. Take care of exorbitant interest obligation
Obligation installments can be a tremendous weight on your general spending plan. In the event that you can take care of exorbitant interest obligation all the more rapidly through additional installments utilizing the snowball or torrential slide techniques, you'll save money on all out revenue paid and free yourself sooner from that weight. Then, begin placing the cash into reserve funds all things considered.

21. Keep reserve funds in a high return investment account
As you pursue your monetary objectives, make a point to put your collecting supports in a high return online bank account to boost your cash. Probably the best internet based accounts pay loan fees that are higher than the ones overall conventional banks.

# Chapter 6

**Try not to restrict your self**

Blog Picture: Don't Restrict Yourself to a Past Private Best
You should comprehend that your outlook influences all that you tell yourself. Your outlook is a finished assortment of your convictions, contemplations and information about yourself and the world you live in. Your mentality is the channel that decides how you get data and respond to it. At the point when quite possibly the most inventive power in the music business of the 20th century was gotten some information about his prosperity, Duke Ellington answered, "I simply took the energy it takes to frown and thought of certain blues." To influence change in your life, transcend any proper mentality of accomplishment and never restrict yourself to your past private best.

To come by various outcomes in your day to day existence, look at the rundown beneath for tips on getting it going:

Nothing is Foreordained - Don't roll together your feelings about things previously. That will just occupy your reasoning and make it difficult to draw out the satisfaction that is as of now holding up inside you.
Hush up and Begin Changing - Whenever you have distinguished a trouble spot that has generally caused you issues, flip the switch and really impact your mentalities to put forth and achieve new objectives.

Develop Self-assurance - Finding your own voice and assuming command over your attitude expects you to be basic about each information yet sure about each choice.

Be Aware..But Get everything rolling - We can all concur that there never is by all accounts sufficient opportunity in a day. The key is to begin utilizing your time all the more admirably.

Never Uncertainty Change is Conceivable - It is essential to pose yourself the right inquiries to reveal negative convictions that might be holding you up.

It's anything but a Race Follow Your Speed - Taking on a development outlook really lessens hostility as you figure out how to depend on your own decisiveness to drive your own accomplishments.

Make the Energy for Good Outcomes - It is not difficult to feel crippled when confronted with affliction. Put resources into your future by giving you a much needed boost and become an individual not entirely set in stone to respond to the call.

Specialists at UCLA found individuals who imagine the course of what should have been finished to address their propensities were bound to take on the propensity than the people who pictured the outcome. For change to stick, you must envision your new propensities. Studies have shown imagining the cycle helps center consideration around what should be finished. The distress that happens when you neglect to satisfy your own assumptions is mental cacophony. It isn't actually to be expected that it sets off a region of the mind that is delicate to torment. You should deal with the uneasiness with your recently procured development mentality.

Blog Picture: Don't Restrict Yourself to a Past Private Best

You actually should comprehend that your attitude influences all that you tell yourself. Your outlook is a finished assortment of your convictions, contemplations and information about yourself and the world you live in. Your mentality is the channel that decides how you get data and respond to it. At the point when perhaps the most imaginative power in the music business of the 20th century had gotten some information about his prosperity, Duke Ellington answered, "I just took the energy it takes to sulk and thought of certain blues." To influence change in your life, transcend any proper outlook of accomplishment and never restrict yourself to your past private best.

If you are somebody who needs to come by various outcomes in your day to day existence, look at the rundown underneath for tips on getting it going:

Nothing is Foreordained - Don't jumble your feelings about things previously. That will just occupy your reasoning and make it difficult to draw out the bliss that is as of now holding up inside you.
Hush up and Begin Changing - Whenever you have distinguished a trouble spot that has generally caused you issues, flip the switch and significantly impact your outlooks to put forth and achieve new objectives.
Develop Self-assurance - Finding your own voice and assuming command over your outlook expects you to be basic about each information yet certain about each choice.
Be Aware..But Get everything rolling - We can all concur that there never is by all accounts sufficient opportunity in a day. The key is to begin utilizing your time all the more shrewdly.

Never Uncertainty Change is Conceivable - It is vital to pose yourself the right inquiries to reveal negative convictions that might be holding you up.
It's anything but a Race Follow Your Speed - Taking on a development outlook really diminishes hostility as you figure out how to depend on your own decisiveness to drive your own accomplishments.
Make the Energy for Good Outcomes - It is not difficult to feel unsettled when confronted with affliction. Put resources into your future by cheering you up and turn into an individual not entirely settled to respond to the call.
Specialists at UCLA found individuals who envision the course of what should have been finished to make progress with their propensities were bound to take on the propensity than the people who imagined the outcome. For change to stick, you should picture your new propensities. Studies have shown picturing the cycle helps center consideration around what should be finished. The distress that happens when you neglect to satisfy your own assumptions is mental discord. It isn't to be expected that it sets off a region of the cerebrum that is delicate to torment. You should deal with the uneasiness with your recently obtained development mentality.

# chapter 7

**Supplicate consistently and have confidence**

One vital motivation to implore is on the grounds that God has instructed us to ask. In the event that we are to be loyal to His will, petitioning heaven should be important for our life in Him.
Christian thinker and researcher Blaise Pascal (1623-62) expressed, "The heart has its reasons of which reason doesn't know anything ... " This article suggests that the request has its reasons. Why we supplicate is significant, as is the petition itself. What I understand are twelve motivations to supplicate.

1. God's Statement Calls Us to Implore

One critical motivation to ask is on the grounds that God has instructed us to implore. In the event that we are to be loyal to His will, petitioning God should be important for our life in Him. Where does the Good book call us to supplication? A few sections are significant:

"Appeal to God for the people who mistreat you" - Matthew 5:44 (NIV) [1]
"Also, when you implore ... " - Matthew 6:5
"This, then, at that point, is the way you ought to supplicate ... " - Matthew 6:9
"Be euphoric in trust, patient in difficulty, dependable in supplication." - Romans 12:12

"What's more, ask in the Soul on all events with a wide range of petitions and demands." - Ephesians 6:18
"Try not to be restless about anything, yet in all things, by supplication and appeal, with thanksgiving, present your solicitations to God." - Philippians 4:6
"Give yourselves to supplication, being careful and grateful." - Colossians 4:2
"Ask consistently" - 1 Thessalonians 5:17
"I encourage, then, above all else, that solicitations, supplications, mediation and thanksgiving be made for everybody ... " - 1 Timothy 2:1
Petitioning God is a demonstration of dutifulness. God calls us to supplicate and we should answer.

2. Jesus Supplicated Routinely

For what reason did Jesus supplicate? One explanation he supplicated was as an illustration with the goal that we could gain from him. The Good news accounts are loaded with references to the requests of Christ, including these models:

"After he had excused them, he went up on a mountainside without help from anyone else to supplicate." - Matthew 14:23
"Then, at that point, Jesus went with his supporters to a spot called Gethsemane, and he shared with them, 'Stay here while I go around there and supplicate.'" - Matthew 26:36
"Promptly in the first part of the day, while it was as yet dim, Jesus got up, went out and headed out to a singular spot, where he supplicated." - Imprint 1:35
"Be that as it may, Jesus frequently pulled out to desolate places and implored." - Luke 5:16

"One of those days Jesus went out to a mountainside to implore, and went through the late evening petitioning God." - Luke 6:12

"Then Jesus advised his trains as an illustration to show them that they ought to constantly ask and not surrender." - Luke 18:1

3. Petitioning God is The manner by which We Speak with God

Petitioning God permits us to love and acclaim the Master. It likewise permits us to offer admission of our wrongdoings, which ought to prompt our veritable apology. In addition, petitioning God awards us the amazing chance to introduce our solicitations to God. These parts of petitioning heaven include correspondence with our Maker. He is private, really focuses on us, and needs to collect with us through petition.

" ... assuming my kin, who are called out to by me, will lower themselves and supplicate and look for my face and abandon their mischievous behavior, then, at that point, will I hear from paradise and will excuse their wrongdoing and will recuperate their property." - 2 Accounts 7:14

Isaiah expressed, "He invigorates the tired and builds the force of the powerless. Indeed, even adolescents become worn out and tired, and young fellows stagger and fall; however the people who trust in the Ruler will reestablish their solidarity. They will take off on wings like hawks; they will run and not develop exhausted, they will walk and not be weak" (Isaiah 40:29-31).

Jews 4:15-16 peruses, "For we don't have an esteemed cleric who can't feel for our shortcomings, yet we have one who has

been enticed inside and out, similarly as we are - yet was without transgression. Allow us then to move toward the privileged position of effortlessness with certainty, so we might get kindness and track down beauty to help us in our period of scarcity."
Petitioning heaven isn't just about requesting God's favors - however we are free to do as such - yet it is about correspondence with the living God. Without correspondence, connections go to pieces. In this way, as well, our relationship with God endures when we don't speak with Him.

4. Petitioning God Permits us to Take part in God's Works

Does God require our assistance? No. He is almighty and in charge of everything in His creation. For what reason do we have to implore? Since petitioning heaven is the means God has appointed for a thing to occur. Supplication, for example, helps other people know the adoration for Jesus. Petitioning God can address human issues far removed for God to work. It isn't so much that God can't work without our requests, however that He has laid out petitioning God as a component of His arrangement for achieving His will in this world.

5. Petitioning God Gives us Control Over Evil

Might actual strength at any point assist us with defeating impediments and difficulties in the profound domain? No, "For our battle isn't against flesh, yet against the rulers, against the specialists, against the powers of this dim world and against the otherworldly powers of malicious in the brilliant domains" (Ephesians 6:12). Yet, in petitioning heaven even the actually frail can major areas of strength for become the profound domain. All things considered, we can call upon God to concede us control over evil.

"For actual preparation is valuable, yet righteousness has an incentive for all things, holding guarantee for both the current life and the life to come." - 1 Timothy 4:8
"Watch and ask so you won't fall into temptation. The soul is willing, yet the body is frail." - Matthew 26:41
6. Petitioning God is Consistently Accessible

This point is canvassed independently in another article. However, one more motivation to implore is on the grounds that request is consistently accessible to us. Nothing can hold us back from moving toward God in petitioning heaven with the exception of our own decisions (Hymn 139:7; Romans 8:38-39).

7. Petitioning heaven Keeps us Humble Before God

Lowliness is a temperance God wants in us (Sayings 11:2; 22:4; Micah 6:8; Ephesians 4:2; James 4:10). Petitioning God advises us that we are not in charge, but rather God is, hence keeping us from pride.

"Accordingly, whoever lowers himself like this kid is the best in the realm of paradise." - Matthew 18:4
8. Petitioning God Awards us the Honor of Encountering God

Through supplication we get an experiential reason for our confidence. We don't overlook the astuteness or purposes behind confidence, however petitioning God makes our experience of God genuine on a close to home level.

9. Addressed Petitioning heaven is a Likely Observer

In the event that our request is replied, it can act as a possible observer for the people who question.

10. Petitioning heaven Fortifies the Connections Between Devotees

Petition fortifies our relationship with God, yet when we ask with different adherents, petitioning God likewise reinforces the connections between individual Christians.

11. Petitioning heaven Can Succeed Where Different Means Have Fizzled

Have every one of your choices been depleted? Petitioning God can succeed where different means have fizzled. Petitioning heaven ought not be a final hotel, yet our most memorable reaction. However, there are times when earnest petitioning for heaven should be presented to achieve something.

12. Petitioning God Satisfies Close to home Requirements

Do we really want God through supplication? Indeed! We were made to work best, inwardly, in a devout relationship with God. As C.S. Lewis put it, "God planned the human machine to run on Himself. He Personally is the fuel our spirits were intended to consume, or the food our spirits were intended to benefit from. There could be no other."

# Chapter 8

**Put stock in God for progress**

These things are in the Word, and God is no respecter of people. What we have today is better than whatever Moses had in the Hebrew Scripture. We can ensure a good outcome. Presently, I'm not saying achievement can continuously be accomplished easily or without exertion, yet we were bound for incredible things.

God made all of us to be something uniquely great, yet I likewise feel that we live in a culture that has completely distorted genuine progress. Actually, I looked into the significance of the word. The American Legacy Word reference (AHD) characterizes accomplishment as "The accomplishment of something wanted, arranged, or endeavored." That is a wide definition. Well, certain individuals are targeting nothing and hitting it without fail. The second definition I found is "The acquiring of distinction or success" (AHD). I can't stand that definition. That is definitely not a genuine meaning of progress by any stretch of the imagination. Heaps of individuals have popularity and flourishing, however they don't have genuine progress.

As I would like to think, achievement should be re-imagined. It's not simply accomplishing something stupendous or enormous. Not every person is called to accomplish something significant, as a matter of fact. I attempt to get this across to our staff constantly. We have 300 individuals on staff here in the U.S. alone, and if not for all of them, we were unable to do what we're called to do. They might in all likelihood never be the one before the camera, however they are as yet a major piece of what we're doing. We truly depend on and value the people who keep our office perfect and looking great. What's more, without the people who keep the streets furrowed and sanded in the colder time of year, we would be in a tough situation. We really want these individuals to assist us with being great stewards of what God has given us. Their positions may not appear to be just about as critical as others, but rather they are unwavering in what God has called them to do. That is the thing I call a triumph. The people who are steadfast in a couple of things will likewise be unwavering in much.

Matthew 25:23 says,

His master said unto him, Great, great and unwavering worker; thou hast been dependable north of a couple of things, I will make you leader over numerous things: enter thou into the delight of thy ruler.

On the off chance that we are great stewards of what God gives us, He'll expand us and give us more. The way that achievement has been introduced is certainly not a faithful idea by any means. I need to empower anybody who feels like they haven't done a lot: God has something else for you, and you can succeed. Your dependability will be compensated. Furthermore, for those of you who believe you're magnificent, I genuinely want to believe that I can assist you with perceiving that achievement did not depend on these brief things that will die. God makes a decision about things uniquely in contrast to what we do.

First Samuel 16:7 says,

For man looketh on the visible presentation, however the Master looketh on the heart.

Many individuals look astounding outwardly, yet in their souls, they're hopeless — they don't enjoy delight or harmony and positively don't have achievement. Grasp this: There isn't anything in this world that will pastor to you or fulfill you more than realizing that you are in the immediate focus of God's will.

Large numbers of you perusing this can't say without a doubt that you realize you're doing what God has called you to do. You might adore God and believe He should utilize you and favor you, yet you don't be aware for sure that you're where you should be. This is one reason individuals are upset and fulfilled. At times, I accept God has given specific individuals a blessed disappointment. He's attempting to work them up. This is one of the manners in which God spurs you and tells you that there's another element.

As per the finesse of God which is given unto me, as a savvy masterbuilder, I have established the groundwork, and another buildeth consequently. In any case, let each man notice how he buildeth immediately. [11] For other establishment can no man lay than that which is laid, which is Jesus Christ. [12] Now assuming any man expand upon this establishment gold, silver, valuable stones, wood, feed, stubble; [13] Each man's work will be made manifest: for the day will announce it, since it will be uncovered by fire; and the fire will attempt each man's work of what sort it is.

1 Corinthians 3:10-13

This is portraying that as we carry on with life, we are either working with gold, silver, and valuable stones or with wood, feed, and stubble. It doesn't say that everyone is working with gold, silver, and valuable stones or that everyone is working with wood, feed, and stubble. We have a decision.

The miserable reality is that large numbers of us construct things in our lives and get things done that aren't what God planned for us.

What's more, we consider these things a triumph. Be that as it may, at some point, we will remain before the Master, and He will put a fire to everything. It says in Matthew 12:36 that we'll give a record of each and every inactive word that we express. Along these lines, God will consider us answerable for each activity and for each word that emerges from our mouths. Anything of wood, roughage, or stubble — regardless of whether it looks great to man and adjusts to the world's norm of progress — is a work of the tissue and will count in vain.

A many individuals think wood, roughage, and stubble are alluding to infidelity, sex, and illicit drug use. Yet, did you had at least some idea that individuals have done things that could seem, by all accounts, to be faithful — began chapels, been in an unfamiliar mission field, and composed love music — yet none of it was driven by God?

For example, my old buddy Arthur Meintjes as of late imparted to me on an episode of Within Story that he once pastored a congregation and later acknowledged he was doing it in his own solidarity. His life turned out to be challenging to the point that he was prepared to end his own life. That is when God showed him beauty and truly turned his life around.

It doesn't make any difference regardless of whether the outcome is great. God believes you should do what He has called you to do, and He maintains that you should do it because of His capacity.

I think what some call burnout is simply individuals doing beneficial things in their own solidarity and power. God's never had anyone qualified working for Him yet, so quit depending on your own capacity. In the event that you have little to no faith in the Ruler, you can't get the things done. He's anticipated you and you won't be genuine .

www.ingramcontent.com/pod-product-compliance
Lightning Source LLC
LaVergne TN
LVHW050340160826
845677LV00014B/3706

* 9 7 9 8 3 5 4 6 4 8 9 7 9 *